YOU CHOOSE

Life in the
MAYA CIVILIZATION

AN INTERACTIVE ANCIENT HISTORY ADVENTURE

BY DANIELLE SMITH-LLERA

Consultant:
Stephanie M. Strauss, Ph.D.
Ancient Mesoamerican
Art and Writing

CAPSTONE PRESS
a capstone imprint

Published by Capstone Press, an imprint of Capstone
1710 Roe Crest Drive, North Mankato, Minnesota 56003
capstonepub.com

Copyright © 2026 by Capstone. All rights reserved. No part of this publication may be reproduced in whole or in part, or stored in a retrieval system, or transmitted in any form or by any means, electronic, mechanical, photocopying, recording, or otherwise, without written permission of the publisher.

Library of Congress Cataloging-in-Publication Data
is available on the Library of Congress website.

ISBN: 9798875216381 (hardcover)
ISBN: 9798875216350 (paperback)
ISBN: 9798875216367 (ebook PDF)

Summary: The Maya Civilization thrived in southeastern Mexico and northern Central America for thousands of years. Its culture was known for its impressive stone buildings and pyramid temples, as well as developments in astronomy and mathematics. But what was it like to live there during the height of this civilization? Explore life in a farming village that faces a devastating volcanic eruption. Help rule a city-state at risk of plunging into war with a rival community. Work as a scribe during a momentous solar eclipse. YOU CHOOSE who to be, where to go, and what to do. Will you succeed? Will you fail? Will you even survive? It's up to you!

Editorial Credits
Editor: Alison Deering; Designer: Bobbie Nuytten;
Media Researcher: Svetlana Zhurkin; Production Specialist: Katy LaVigne

Image Credits
Getty Images: Arctic-Images, 24, Federica Grassi, 34, Stringer/Joern Haufe, 103; The Metropolitan Museum of Art: Anonymous Gift, 2005, 55, Gift of Charles and Valerie Diker, 1999, 52, The Crosby Brown Collection of Musical Instruments, 1889, cover (bottom left), The Michael C. Rockefeller Memorial Collection, Bequest of Nelson A. Rockefeller, 1979, 31; Shutterstock: Aleksandr Medvedkov, 4, Andreas Wolochow, 44, Aninka Bongers-Sutherland, 61, CK-TravelPhotos, 97, Diego Grandi, 66, 82, Donnebryant, 8, 14, 40, 70, 100, DRONDPQ, 75, Ingo Bartussek, cover (middle), Leonid Andronov, 108, Lucy. Brown, 105, maradon 333 (stone doorway), cover, 1, Mel Gonzalez, 78, Peter Versnel, 87, Sidhe, 6–7 (base map), SL-Photography, 109, TLF Images, 12, WH_Pics, 73, WitR, 11

Any additional websites and resources referenced in this book are not maintained, authorized, or sponsored by Capstone. All product and company names are trademarks™ or registered® trademarks of their respective holders.

Printed and bound in China. 6276

TABLE OF CONTENTS

ABOUT YOUR ADVENTURE............... 5
**GET TO KNOW
  THE MAYA CIVILIZATION** 6

Chapter 1
GAME OF THE GODS 9

Chapter 2
AN ANGRY MOUNTAIN 15

Chapter 3
FRIEND OR FOE? 41

Chapter 4
THE DARKEST SHADOW................71

Chapter 5
GIFTS FROM THE MAYA 101

Timeline of the Maya Civilization 106
More About the Maya Civilization 107
The Maya Civilization Today 108
Glossary 110
Read More 111
Internet Sites 111
About the Author 112
Books in This Series 112

ABOUT YOUR ADVENTURE

YOU are a proud citizen of the Maya Civilization. Life is full of celebrations, family gatherings, and storytelling—these are among the many ways your civilization feels connected. But war and natural disasters are also a part of life.

You could be facing an active volcano in Joya de Cerén, a farming village in the Zapotitán Valley. Or you might be living in Tikal, a powerful and independent city-state, preparing for an attack from a rival. Or you could be facing a frightening solar eclipse in Palenque.

Wherever you are, YOU CHOOSE which path to take. Will you survive? Or will you and your community be destroyed?

Turn the page to begin your adventure.

Get to Know
THE MAYA CIVILIZATION

The Maya Civilization was divided into city-states. They traded with each other, formed alliances, and battled for territory. Each city-state also had its own government, laws, and army.

Each Maya city-state was led by an ajaw—a religious leader with a special connection to the gods.

An aj k'uhun—or priest—was a title for those believed to have a special power to heal others and communicate with the spirit world.

The Maya valued astronomy—the study of stars, planets, and other objects in space. They used this to decide when to plant and harvest crops. Astronomy was also thought to carry special messages from the gods. For example, the Maya believed that Chak Ek—the planet Venus—influenced rainfall, war, and other crucial parts of life. They based aspects of their calendar on its movement.

A codex is an accordion-style book that the Maya used to record history, astronomy, religious stories, and other valuable information about ancient Maya life.

A huipil was a loose shirt worn by women in ancient Maya cities. The huipil continues to be worn by Maya women today and often features colorful designs unique to their region or specific village.

The Maya extracted sticky resin from copal trees to make incense. This was burned during religious ceremonies.

A windowless room full of steam—called a pibnaah—was where the Maya headed to rest, heal from sickness, prepare for a ceremony, and even to give birth.

Hun Hunahpu—one of the Maya's most important gods—controlled the corn harvest. He was depicted with a long head like an ear of corn and fine hair like corn silk.

Corn was a main food source for the Maya. It was often ground into flour to make waj, a bread similar to tortillas.

Maya cooks used a grinding stone and a flat, sloping stone called metate to turn grains, roots, and seeds into flour.

An enormous network of paved roads—called sacbe—connected Maya towns and villages. Their slightly raised designs made the sacbe usable even during the rainy season. These roads are still greatly admired by modern-day engineers.

The ancient Maya ball game of pitz—also called pok ta pok in some regions—has been played for sport and as a religious ceremony for roughly 3,000 years.

MAP KEY
- ○ Maya historical site
- ▨ valley
- ▨ Maya Civilization

○ Palenque   ○ Tikal

Life-size portraits of Maya rulers carved on stone slabs called stelae can still be found standing at Maya archaeological sites.

The Maya believed the dead traveled through a frightening watery Underworld called Xibalba. This land also had other names depending on the region.

Zapotitán Valley
Joya de Cerén ○

Yaxtuun—jade stone—represented growth and life for the Maya. Its green color reminded them of plants and water.

Chapter 1
GAME OF THE GODS

Smack! A ball bounces off a hip or knee. Players wearing headdresses crafted from leather, fur, and feathers hustle across a stone court. The court is carved with skulls, jaguars, and other Maya religious symbols.

Two teams lunge and dive after a heavy ball made with sticky sap from rubber trees in the nearby forest. Spectators cheer—but they also watch anxiously. This game, an important part of Maya culture, is a ceremony. If players score points by keeping the ball in motion, the gods are pleased. But if they play without skill, the gods may punish their community with a drought or other natural disaster.

For thousands of years, the Maya Civilization thrived in parts of eastern Mexico, Guatemala, El Salvador, Honduras, and Belize.

The earliest settlements, which date from 1800 BCE, grew into a civilization that flourished in the southern region until the 900s CE. After 1000 CE, communities in the northern region began to thrive.

The Maya were an advanced civilization. They built roads to link cities, towns, and villages. They gathered in marketplaces to trade food, crafts, and ideas. They were farmers, artists, mathematicians, storytellers, musicians, priests, astronomers, and architects. They were also scribes. The Maya created a complex writing system. They used it to keep records and calendars that organized their lives.

But the Maya were not ruled by one leader. They lived in small kingdoms called city-states. Each one was ruled by an ajaw and had its own government, laws, and army. Each city-state also had a main city where people gathered

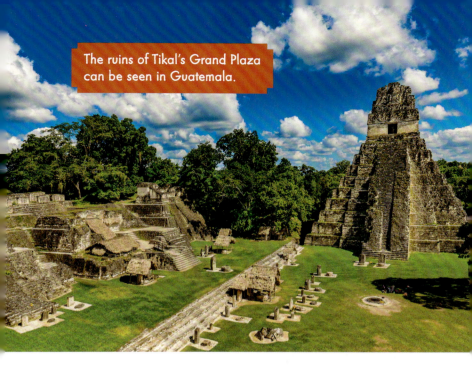

The ruins of Tikal's Grand Plaza can be seen in Guatemala.

for ceremonies, festivals, and ball games. These events offered city-states—which often engaged in battles for territory—the chance to form alliances, avoid war, and maintain their power. For centuries, the city-state of Tikal, located in modern-day Guatemala, was the most powerful. Its grand temples, palaces, and plazas were once home to tens of thousands of residents.

The Maya believed their gods—at least 200 of them—controlled every part of life, from weather to war. Droughts, hurricanes, earthquakes, volcanic eruptions—in mountainous places like the Zapotitán Valley—and other natural disasters were signs that the gods were angry. Even solar eclipses meant that humans had done something to upset them. The Maya held ceremonies in attempts to maintain peace. Carvings found on the stone

Maya carvings in Palenque, located in modern-day Mexico, were once colorfully painted.

buildings of Palenque, a city-state located in modern-day Mexico, are extraordinary examples of how the Maya used art and architecture to honor their powerful gods.

How would you handle life in the Maya Civilization? Would you be able to escape a volcanic eruption if you were living in Joya de Cerén, a village in the rich farming area of the Zapotitán Valley? Would you be able to help your royal cousin stop an enemy attack if you were living in the powerful city-state of Tikal? Would you know how to handle a frightening solar eclipse if you were training as a scribe, tasked with copying important documents by hand, in the city-state of Palenque? Make a choice to find out!

To experience life in Joya de Cerén during a volcanic eruption, turn to page 15.

To experience life in Tikal, helping your royal cousin stop an enemy attack, turn to page 41.

To experience Mayan life in Palenque, training as scribe and facing a solar eclipse, turn to page 71.

Chapter 2
AN ANGRY MOUNTAIN

Mountains tower over your farming village in the Zapotitán Valley. The soil of Joya de Cerén is rich thanks to nearby volcanoes that long ago spewed rocks and ash across the valley. Outside the adobe buildings, cornstalks stand tall in the fields. Tomorrow the whole village will head to the fields for the harvest. But tonight, everyone will give thanks to Hun Hunahpu, the corn god.

You hurry inside the ceremony hall and squeeze onto a bench between your mother and father. Your twin baby brothers, Hunahpu and Xbalanque, bounce on your parents' laps. They are named after hero twins who defeated gods in a ball game.

Turn the page.

In the center of the hall, a priest wearing a deer-antler headdress dances to the rhythm of rattles and wooden drums. People sway to the music. The ceremony sends a message of thanks to Hun Hunahpu for the rich harvest.

Suddenly, the ground rumbles deeply below your feet. Cabrakán, the god of the mountains, is angry! It's not unusual for earthquakes to shake the valley, but today, the walls rattle more violently than usual.

Everyone rushes outside. Looking around the plaza, you are relieved. The terrible shaking of the ground has stopped. No buildings have collapsed. But your relief is short-lived.

"Cabrakán's anger is only just beginning!" the priest shouts. He points to the mountaintop, where a strange gray cloud is rising.

You've heard stories about the valley's quiet volcanoes suddenly erupting in the past. They have destroyed villages and killed thousands of your ancestors. Your town is directly in the path of the one towering over your village.

You stare in horror at the gray cloud. It is rising faster and faster from the volcano. There isn't much time. Your town is directly in the shadow of the volcano.

Your heart pounds with terror. All around you, people are rushing to escape the plaza. You turn, looking desperately for your parents and brothers. But you've been separated in the crowd!

It's possible they went home. You decide to look for them there. Rushing along the path toward your house, you feel the earth lurch beneath your feet. You are hurled to the ground. From behind a neighbor's house, you hear a loud commotion. It could be someone in need of help. What should you do?

To continue toward home, turn to page 18.
To stop and check on the noise, turn to page 31.

You need to find your family, but when you reach home, no one is here. You spot stone axes resting in their usual spot by the door. Your family uses them to cut wood from the nearby forest. The wood feeds the fires in the village's stoves, even the one in the public sweat bath next door.

Just then, the ground lurches again! You drop to your knees as grass from the shaking roof falls around you. Cracks spread across the adobe walls, but the wood frames inside keep your house standing.

You stumble to the doorway. Next door, you spot the dome-shaped roof of the public sweat bath. Its thick walls might protect you from the lava the volcano will spew when it erupts. But fleeing the village might be safer—if you make it out in time. What do you do next?

To seek shelter inside the sweat bath, turn to page 19.

To flee the village, turn to page 21.

You drop to your hands and knees and crawl to the sweat bath. The entrance is very small to keep warm, moist air trapped inside. Villagers come here to rest after a long day. It's also a place to heal from sickness.

In the center of the floor, coals glow under a stack of large rocks. You feel calm and safe in this familiar space.

You reach for a jug of water sitting near the coals. Painted on its clay surface is the body of a serpent with feathers. It's Tohil, the god of fire.

You pour the water over the heated rocks. Steam quickly fills the room. It wraps around you like a warm blanket. You feel peaceful—until you hear rattling above. The volcano must be belching rocks across the village.

You stare at the coiled shape of Tohil on the clay jug. Fire is a wonderful gift from nature. It can make life better, like the relaxing steam in

Turn the page.

this room. But it can also destroy, like the heat trapped inside the volcano waiting to get out.

Nature has two sides to balance each other. This is the lesson you've heard often from the elders. You crouch in the darkness, wondering if you'll survive nature's terrifying side.

Through the walls, you hear a roar rise from the volcano. Seconds later, the dome ceiling cracks above you. A great blob of orange lava has broken through like a giant fist.

Burning heat fills the sweat bath. You breathe your last breath and wonder if your family will escape the volcano's destruction. As your spirit begins its journey to the Xibalba, land of the dead, you feel relieved that so many ancestors will be waiting there to welcome you.

THE END

To follow another path, turn to page 13.
To learn more about the Maya Civilization,
turn to page 101.

Standing in the doorway, you stare up at the volcano. Tiny rocks shower down and sting your eyes. You know it's time to leave the village.

You quickly step back into the house and begin filling a basket with sharp stone axes and blades. Any village needs wood for its cooking fires or to strengthen adobe walls. These tools could help your family start a new life somewhere far from the volcano.

You heave the basket onto your back, then place the strap across your forehead to help carry the load. You start toward the door, but your knees wobble with each step and you drop the basket. You won't be able to take it after all.

You look around, desperate to bring your family something from the home. Finally, you settle for the blankets on the grass sleeping mats.

Turn the page.

Hugging the colorful woven cotton to your chest, you run outside. Larger rocks are now raining down from the volcano. They feel like sharp blades as they bounce off your skin.

You merge into the mass of people racing out of town. They hold terrified children and help carry the oldest villagers. There is no way to find your family in the chaos—you must focus on simply getting away from the danger. You hope they are somewhere among the crowd.

Much of the crowd seems to be heading for the sacbe, the paved road outside of town. But there is also a smaller group racing toward the river. Jumping into a canoe could offer a faster escape. Which direction will you choose?

To head to the river, turn to page 23.
To follow the crowd to the paved road, turn to page 25.

You rush to the riverbank where fishermen have pulled up their canoes. The cool smell of the water soothes you—but not for long.

The most powerful earthquake yet rumbles beneath your feet, throwing you to the ground. You land on the riverbank and stare down into the water. A dark, terrifying world stares back at you. You've heard stories about underwater tunnels leading to Xibalba, the land of death. A new terror washes over you. Is this where this river will lead you?

A roar suddenly drowns out the river. A blob of lava lands near you, giving off intense heat. It glows orange under a black crust.

More lava hisses through the air as it falls around you. Squinting through the trees, you see people rushing along the paved road. But two figures are standing still—your parents!

Before you can call out to them, a ball of lava splashes into the river next to you. An

Turn the page.

explosion of deadly steam is triggered as the molten lava meets the water.

A blast of air wraps you in burning heat, and you know it's too late to escape. You will never again enjoy the sweat bath's soothing warmth or tend its fire with your family. But in your last moments, you feel relief that they are on the road to safety.

THE END

To follow another path, turn to page 13.
To learn more about the Maya Civilization,
turn to page 101.

You hurry toward the paved road. Crews from your village have built it expertly. Plaster layered over rocks creates a smooth, hard surface. The road—called a sacbe—leads into the forest and makes a short platform. Even when rain brings mud and puddles, it's easy to walk to other villages and even faraway cities.

As you rush along with the crowd, you hear your name. Spinning around, you see your parents! They throw their arms around you.

"We're all in this together," your father says.

There is no time to say more. The earth jerks back and forth, more violently now. The road feels rubbery as you run alongside your family. Two people hurry by carrying an old woman between them. No one will be left behind.

With a great roar, the volcano erupts. Everyone stops to listen with shock. The forest around you is so dense, you cannot see what's

Turn the page.

happening to your village. But you don't want to—you could not bear seeing its destruction.

Families set up small camps along the road to rest. Tomorrow morning, you will all complete the journey to the nearest town.

"Thank you for bringing these blankets," says your mother, wrapping one around your brothers. "But getting separated from you was terrifying."

She wraps the other blanket around your shoulders. Your family soon falls asleep, but you are restless. You can't stop thinking about lava falling on your village.

Nearby, a group of people huddles around the glow of a fire. Farther away, you hear someone playing a flute. Where do you go?

To follow the sound of the flute, turn to page 27.
To follow the glow of the fire, turn to page 29.

You follow the sound of the music and come upon an aj k'uhun, or priest. She is playing a sad melody on her clay flute. Back in the village, music and plant medicine were important parts of her healing ceremonies. She helps care for people's bodies and their emotions.

You notice a small deerskin pouch around her waist. You know it contains stones that help the aj k'uhun make predictions. You're impatient for her to use them.

As if she heard your thoughts, she sets down her flute and empties the pouch of stones into her hand. She scatters them on the ground and studies the pattern. You hold your breath.

"In the future, I see a group of strangely dressed people. Most look like us," she says looking at the stones with a faraway expression. "They carry tools to carve through

Turn the page.

volcanic ash hardened into rock. They will discover the pots full of beans, woven blankets, and even our footprints in the gardens that we just left behind. They will be eager to learn about us because we are their ancestors."

It's strange to think about being someone's ancestor when you're only 12 years old. There is also sadness knowing your village—the only home you've ever known—is lost. But you feel a strange happiness knowing that so many people you'll never meet will care about what happened in your village today. Your story will not end here.

THE END

To follow another path, turn to page 13.
To learn more about the Maya Civilization, turn to page 101.

You make your way to the fire and enjoy the relaxing warmth. But you wish you were back in the sweat bath washing the gritty volcanic ash off your skin.

Cries of terror jolt you from the peaceful moment. You look around in a panic and see a pale figure emerging from the dark forest. Like a ghost, it slowly moves toward the fire.

As the figure moves closer, you breathe a sigh of relief—it's a man. Gray powder covers his hair, skin, and clothing. It must be ash spewed by the volcano.

"I'm the last one to leave the village," he says. "The ash fell so fast. The piles climbed up the walls of our houses, the tree trunks in the plaza, and the cornstalks in our fields. When I looked back from the road, I saw what the volcano had done. In just a few hours, ash turned our village, the green fields, and forest into a gray desert."

Turn the page.

Tears fill your eyes. When you rub them, you feel the grit of volcanic ash. It's falling here too and probably across the whole valley. You wonder how far everyone will have to travel to escape the volcano's destruction.

"I helped build this road," the man says in a stronger voice. "Its surface is made with volcanic rock created by another eruption long ago. Now it will take us to safety and a new life."

You look over at the pale road glowing in the darkness with some pride. But you know decades—maybe centuries—will pass before anyone calls this latest volcanic eruption a gift from nature.

THE END

To follow another path, turn to page 13.
To learn more about the Maya Civilization,
turn to page 101.

You decide to investigate. When you enter the storehouse behind your neighbor's home, you see a duck flying wildly. The pet lives happily here, laying eggs, snapping up insects and fallen food. The shaking earth has alarmed her, but she doesn't fly out the open doorway.

You scan the clay pots stacked along the walls. They are full of beans, corn, chilies, and many other dried foods that provide meals year-round. You quickly choose some supplies.

A figurine of Hun Hunahpu, the Maya corn god

You fill a sack of manioc flour. Manioc roots are poisonous. But when soaked, squeezed, dried, and ground into flour, they make bread that hardly spoils. You also grab a small pot of dried cacao seeds, a valuable item

Turn the page.

to trade in markets. When mixed with chili peppers, the powder makes a chocolate drink so special that nobles and royalty drink it in faraway cities like Tikal and Palenque.

Suddenly the ground jerks under your feet. A stack of pots tumbles toward you. You feel the heavy clay crack against your head. The room spins and you drop to the ground.

When you come to, the duck has flown away—you know you should too.

Clutching your bleeding head, you stagger outside. The falling rocks sting your skin, so you stumble into the farmhouse. You spot sleeping mats and cotton blankets. You feel too dizzy to run or even walk—maybe you should lay down. But maybe it's too late for that now. Do you take a short rest or keep stumbling toward the doorway?

To lay down, turn to page 33.
To keep going, turn to page 34.

You climb up the sleeping platform to lie down—just for a moment. As you slip off to sleep, a great roar rumbles deep underground. The volcano has erupted, but it seems far away. You are dreaming about a green field where the whole village is picking ripe corn in the sun.

You wake up, coughing violently. The roof above you has caved in. Ash is falling in a thick shower all around you.

You leap off the sleeping platform and into the deep gray powder. Your feet sink into the gritty ash when you try to walk. Panic fills you with energy, but there is nowhere to go. Ash is burying the whole village—and soon it will bury you. As the ash piles up higher and higher around your body, you try to convince yourself that you're still dreaming.

THE END

To follow another path, turn to page 13.
To learn more about the Maya Civilization, turn to page 101.

With a volcano rumbling, you know there is no time to waste! But you're so dizzy that the cozy room feels like a dream.

A delicious smell fills the air. Chili peppers, beans, and squash have been cooked into a rich stew. The clay cooking pot rests on three large stones over hot coals—like your stove at home and in all the homes you've ever visited.

You know you should be leaving, but you pause at the stone tool—a metate—where corn has been ground into flour. When mixed with water, patted into discs, and roasted over fire, it becomes a flatbread called waj that feeds your people.

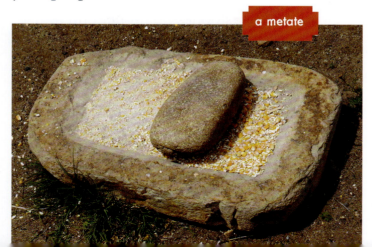

a metate

A deafening roar brings you back to reality. The volcano has erupted!

You scramble toward the doorway. On impulse, you grab a small pot that holds burning incense from the copal tree. The smoke sends a message to the gods asking for a good harvest.

The air outside the house feels so cold—even as sizzling lumps of lava land on the ground. Looking up, you see ash is rising from the volcano. It reaches so high it threatens to block the sun. You are terrified by Cabrakán's fury and power.

You hear shouts from the plaza. Is that your father's voice? You can't be sure. Should you go investigate? Or maybe it's safer to run across the fields surrounding the village to the road outside of town.

> To run toward the road, turn to page 36.
> To run toward the plaza, turn to page 38.

Racing behind the farmhouse toward the road, your eyes sting. Gritty bits of volcanic ash are getting into them.

As you run through the field, your feet sink into the rich soil. The rain god, Chaac, has been generous, striking the clouds with his lightning ax to release showers all summer. If only Cabrakán, the mountain god, weren't sending this shower of ash! It's falling so thickly now that it makes you cough and burns your throat.

You run past squash plants, bean vines winding up corn stalks, orange-brown pods hanging in cacao trees, and cotton plants—all dusted in gray. Even the manioc plants are being slowly buried. They can survive droughts, but not a gray ash desert.

Finally, through the cloudy air, you see the road up ahead—and your family! As people rush around them, your parents stand still, looking around desperately. Your brothers cry with fear.

As you run toward them, your mind rushes ahead to a new danger—one that has nothing to do with lava or ash. You have nothing packed for the long journey ahead. You've left behind cooking pots full of tonight's dinner—as well as storehouses and fields full of food. What will happen when everyone gets hungry? You'll look out for your own family, just like everyone else. Hunger and desperation could break apart a community that once shared food, stories, celebrations, and ancestors.

You clutch the small clay pot closer. You'll burn copal incense and ask the gods for help with the sweet smoke. You and everyone on the road are going to need it.

THE END

To follow another path, turn to page 13.
To learn more about the Maya Civilization,
turn to page 101.

You race toward the plaza. It feels like madness to be running toward the volcano, but you're sure you heard your father's voice.

Moments later, you spot him in the gloom. The ash streaking your father's face and hair make him look like a much older man.

"We must go!" he says. "Cabrakán's fury is great—lava is flowing down the mountain!"

Together, you rush past stalls set up for serving food at the harvest celebration. They are all empty. The village already seems inhabited by ghosts.

Under the plaza trees, your ankle twists as you slip on a fallen avocado. Stumbling into your father, you fall to the ground. One of your father's legs twists painfully beneath him.

You watch helplessly as the incense pot slips from your hand and shatters. You quickly grab the precious chunk of copal incense from the broken pieces.

"The lava is falling faster!" your father shouts, pushing you to your feet. "Run! Your mother and brothers are waiting on the road. Don't look back!"

"I'm not leaving without you!" you insist.

You help your father stand. He winces in pain but drapes an arm across your shoulders. Together, you limp through the maze of cooling lava piles covering the plaza.

You know that speed will not save you as lava blobs steadily fall. You squeeze the chunk of copal incense and pray the gods reward your bravery with survival. Your only comfort is knowing that you and your father will face any fate together, even if that means limping together into Xibalba, the land of the dead.

THE END

To follow another path, turn to page 13.
To learn more about the Maya Civilization, turn to page 101.

Chapter 3
FRIEND OR FOE?

Tikal's wide plaza is often crowded with people attending ceremonies. But today it's so quiet, you can hear the jungle buzzing with insects.

"I think I see a quetzal over there in the trees, Itzel," you say to your cousin. Back at the palace, she has a headdress made of the bird's long blue-green tail feathers.

Itzel is too busy studying a tall stone slab to respond. It's carved with the life-size image of her father, a famous king of Tikal. He wears rich clothing and jewelry.

Itzel touches the elegant lines of writing cut into the stone. They tell of her father's great leadership and bravery. He died when she was a young child. Soon after, she became the next ajaw—the queen of Tikal.

Turn the page.

"What will be carved on mine?" Itzel asks. She studies the row of stones, each representing a ruler. They all helped Tikal become powerful and wealthy.

"You don't have to worry about that now," you say.

But you know Itzel cannot forget her responsibilities. For years, nobles have been teaching her about how to protect and rule Tikal. The city-state has thrived under a long line of powerful rulers for centuries. Itzel must feel tremendous pressure to keep Tikal's dominant position.

Itzel is also learning that she must speak directly to the gods. It's a power granted to an ajaw. This summer, when crops withered, Itzel helped lead a ceremony in this plaza to honor the rain god, Chaac. When showers came, you felt so relieved—Tikal would see your cousin as an ajaw with real powers.

"My advisors say that an ajaw behaves like a tree," says Itzel, standing up and stretching her arms up toward the sky. "Like branches reaching toward the sky, I must keep Tikal safe by honoring the gods and earning their protection. I must also keep Tikal stable—like roots that keep a tree from toppling over."

Now your cousin leans forward. Her face looks suddenly grown-up and serious.

"I came here because I need my father's spirit for strength," she whispers. "Guards have captured a spy from Calakmul, our greatest rival. He was found spying inside one of our weapons storage rooms. He admitted that Calakmul's warriors are preparing to attack us—again. Their ball games are now practice for real battles."

You understand Itzel's concern. Tikal and Calakmul have gone to war for years. Her father died in battle with the rival city-state.

Turn the page.

"I know what will be carved on your stone, cousin," you say. "Queen Itzel ended war with Calakmul once and for all!"

Itzel's face grows serious. "Do you think we should prepare the army and strike first?"

You hesitate. Striking first would

A tall stone slab shows a Maya ajaw.

put Tikal in the strongest position. But maybe there is a way to avoid war this time. What advice do you give your cousin?

To advise Itzel to prepare the army, go to page 45.

To advise Itzel to avoid war, turn to page 62.

"Tikal is bigger and stronger than it's ever been," you tell Itzel. "Our warriors are ready. Calakmul will see that going to battle with Tikal was a huge mistake."

You and Itzel are at the palace—a collection of grand buildings and temples painted deep red and connected by stairs and ramps. The platform you stand on rises high above the city. The setting sun glows orange on the plazas, ball courts, works, homes, gardens, and fields.

"You are right, cousin," says Itzel. "Tikal must behave like the jaguar. We will launch a surprise ambush."

"We have weapons as sharp as jaguar's claws!" you add.

Traders regularly bring spear tips and knife blades made of obsidian—a glossy, black volcanic rock—to Tikal's large market. They are so sharp that just a touch can cut skin.

Turn the page.

But you suddenly feel a pang of worry. Jaguars live and hunt alone. People rely on their families and communities—like coyotes. Your people admire this dog-like animal, even though it is small and weak compared to a jaguar. The coyote is clever and knows how to work with a pack.

Thinking of the coyote makes you wonder if it's wise for Tikal to attack Calakmul alone. Perhaps you should seek support from another city-state. But waiting means Tikal's army might lose the opportunity for a surprise ambush. Do you advise your cousin to gather Tikal's allies or act now?

> To suggest sending warriors to Calakmul immediately, turn to page 47.
>
> To urge Itzel to seek support from allies, turn to page 49.

"Calakmul's warriors are in for a surprise," you tell Itzel the next morning as she prepares to send Tikal's army into battle.

Your cousin nods, and you notice how much she looks like an ajaw. Her headdress of quetzal feathers and jewelry made of jade—a precious stone as green as new leaves or fresh corn husks—make her seem like one of the gods.

The rhythm of drums and rattles matches the steady beat of warriors marching across the plaza below. Dressed in thick armor woven from cotton, they carry weapons made of wood and stone.

"These warriors will join those already posted at our fortress in the forest. They will wait for the enemy there," says Itzel. She glances down at her red throne carved to look like a jaguar. Its eyes are sparkling stones, and its sharp fangs are white shells. "Like a jaguar, our attack will be quiet and deadly."

Turn the page.

You smile proudly at your cousin's confidence. Then you hear an advisor's whisper rise in alarm. He rushes over to Itzel.

"A messenger has arrived from the fortress, your highness," the advisor begins. "He is wounded but was able to make it here to warn us. Calakmul forces have ambushed the small group of warriors posted there."

Itzel's trembling headdress shows her fear. "Now Calakmul forces will be lying in wait for our soldiers," she whispers.

Itzel's advisors are rushing over. But to regain her confidence as a leader, you believe she needs a special kind of help. She could climb the highest temple to speak to the gods. Or you could suggest she visit her father's tomb to speak to his spirit. Where do you urge your cousin to turn for advice?

To urge Itzel to speak to the gods, turn to page 51.
To suggest Itzel go visit her father's tomb, turn to page 54.

"Remember, cousin, these advisors allowed your father to face Calakmul alone," you tell Itzel outside the royal hall. "It cost him his life. Tikal needs its allies."

Itzel nods and walks into the hall lit by burning pinewood torches. Her advisors are inside preparing to discuss military strategy. You wait anxiously to hear their plan.

Finally, your cousin emerges. "Messengers are heading north to Uaxactun to speak with the ajaw," she says. "They will remind him that Calakmul is a threat to the entire region."

"That's great news!" you say. "Uaxactun is our neighbor and our ally."

But Itzel looks anxious. "Uaxactun's warriors will join our army, but who will lead it?" she asks. "My father led his warriors into battle himself."

Itzel is right. Her father did lead warriors into battle. But he was captured, taken back to

Turn the page.

Calakmul, and—like most any defeated ajaw—sacrificed in a ceremony to honor the gods. You are horrified to think this could happen to Itzel.

"You should be nowhere near the battlefield," you say. A young ajaw without war experience would be an easy and highly valuable prisoner for the enemy.

Your cousin is determined to be a brave and bold leader—and you are determined to keep her safe. If you remind her that she won't be able to serve Tikal if she's killed in battle, she may stay back. Or you could offer to travel with the army as her representative and report back from the battlefield. Do you try to reason with your cousin or volunteer for a dangerous mission?

> To remind Itzel of the risks she faces, turn to page 57.
>
> To volunteer to travel with Tikal's army, turn to page 59.

Your cousin bravely leads the way to the top of one of Tikal's highest pyramids. Looking down, you feel dizzy.

"Once the gods are on our side, we'll defeat Calakmul," you tell Itzel. "Are you nervous about the ceremony?"

Itzel nods. "I am, cousin," she says softly. "I've never done this before. I can't afford to make any mistakes."

You focus on Itzel's deerskin sandals climbing ahead of you. Up here in the sky, you feel as if you've traveled to another world. The gods of war have beautiful names like Ah-Cun-Can and Buluc-Chabtan. But their frightening images fill your imagination. You've heard stories about their snarling faces, jaguar claws, scorpion tails, and headdresses made of snakes. They carry spears, shields, and burning torches. These gods are reminders that war is frightening and violent.

Turn the page.

Finally, you reach the flat platform at the top of the pyramid. Itzel's headdress shimmers against the red of the temple. She lights copal incense. You stand near the priests gathered around her but look away. You're nervous to watch your cousin do something so important.

A small gasp makes you look back. Itzel is holding an obsidian blade—a drop of blood falls from her tongue onto the floor, followed by another. Your cousin's expression is so serious it could be carved into stone.

An artifact shows a Maya ajaw wearing a large headdress and jade beads.

"The gods will be honored by this sacrifice!" a nobleman cries. "This royal blood honors our warriors spilling their blood in battle."

The sight of the blood coming from your cousin's mouth makes you feel faint. The edges of your vision go black, and then you see blue sky as you tip back into the empty air. The only thing waiting to catch you will be the ground far, far below.

Suddenly hands grab onto your shirt and pull you back onto the platform. Itzel and a group of priests kneel around you. You're so relieved to be alive—and to know that Itzel won't have to face ruling Tikal without you. The gods have spared your life. You can only hope they'll be as generous with the warriors marching off to battle.

THE END

To follow another path, turn to page 13.
To learn more about the Maya Civilization,
turn to page 101.

"Your father's spirit—and the ancestors—will guide you in this war with Calakmul," you tell Itzel as you sit together on the steps of the pyramid built over her father's tomb.

"I'm going to need all the help I can get," she says, examining her face in a small, round mirror made of polished stone. "I forget how young I am—I think others do too."

As the last of the sunset reflects off the mirror, you think about the sun starting its journey into the land of the dead—called Metnal in your region. It travels like a jaguar, able to see in the dark, through the night.

A rustle in the forest brings you back to the present.

"What's over there?" Itzel whispers.

You follow her anxious gaze to a nearby tangle of plants. Are those a pair of gleaming eyes? Before you can be sure, they disappear into the shadows.

"The evening light is playing tricks," you say. "We should hurry—night will come soon."

In a small stone bowl, Itzel lights chunks of copal incense. You hope the sweet smoke will please her father's spirit. You can picture his tomb beneath the pyramid. The room would be painted to show important events from your uncle's life. It must be full of his favorite objects, including cups for drinking chocolate.

a Maya drinking cup

You've heard spirits face many challenges in the land of the dead—crossing jagged mountains and rivers of blood, escaping flying obsidian knives. That is why an ajaw is buried with jade masks—to show their power and wealth—as well as weapons, food, and even a clay dog for company on the journey.

Turn the page.

Just then a moving shape at the base of the pyramid catches your eye. A jaguar has stepped out of the forest! Its eyes are fixed on Itzel, who is busy praying near the bowl of incense.

For a moment, you believe Itzel's father has taken its form. But then you see the animal's muscles tighten under its gold-and-black spotted fur. The animal is poised to strike.

"Get out of here, Itzel!" you shout as you dive between her and certain death.

The jaguar's breath is hot on your face as it closes in. You only hope that Itzel doesn't wait long before she lights copal incense to call you back from the Metnal for a visit.

THE END

To follow another path, turn to page 13.
To learn more about the Maya Civilization,
turn to page 101.

"When Tikal conquers Calakmul, that will be carved onto your stone," you tell Itzel. "And you'll keep the carvers very busy recording many accomplishments in your long life. But only if you stay safe. Do not go into battle yourself. You will be the enemy's prime target. If you are killed, Tikal loses its ajaw."

Reluctantly, your cousin agrees. Days later, you stand together on a high platform, watching Tikal's warriors march out of the plaza toward Uaxactun to gather more warriors.

A noble suddenly rushes up the stairs and speaks quietly to Itzel. Your cousin shakes her head at what she's hearing. But then she lifts her chin under her quetzal feather headdress.

"Calakmul warriors have joined forces with the nearby kingdom of Waka, which is small but powerful," Itzel announces. "They'll reach our army before it meets up with Uaxactun's warriors. We'll be outnumbered."

Turn the page.

"You must flee," you urge. "Go into hiding!"

Itzel straightens her shoulders under the jaguar fur cape that once belonged to her father. "My father never fled the battlefield," she reminds you. "Our army must not flee either."

Days later, news finally comes. Tikal was fighting a losing battle when Uaxactun's warriors arrived—just in time. They launched a surprise attack and helped defeat Calakmul and Waka.

You're overjoyed that your cousin has escaped her father's fate—death by an obsidian blade in a public ceremony in Calakmul—at least for now.

THE END

To follow another path, turn to page 13.
To learn more about the Maya Civilization,
turn to page 101.

"I will travel with the army," you tell Itzel. "I'll represent you and be your eyes and ears."

Itzel reluctantly gives you permission. A few days later, you are preparing to march out of the city with the army when she surprises you with a gift—a collection of small figures made of colorful thread. Children share their worries with these tiny dolls at bedtime, making it easier to go to sleep.

"I guess we're not too old for these," you say, realizing how many worries you both carry. "Thank you, cousin. I'll be back soon with news of Tikal's victory."

You wish you felt as confident as you sound. Messengers have warned that Calakmul's forces are drawing closer to Tikal by the moment.

The army travels through the forest toward one of Tikal's fortresses hidden in the trees. Uaxactun's forces will meet you there.

Turn the page.

The wooden watchtower finally appears. Deep trenches have been dug all around it. When the warriors climb down into them, they are as well-hidden among the leaves and shadows as a jaguar with spotted fur.

Inside the fortress, you slip between the warriors. They are preparing their weapons and armor for battle. You crouch down and try to be invisible, wondering how you can be useful when Calakmul's forces try to raid the fortress. You feel exhausted by the stress, not to mention the long march. Sitting against the stone wall, you rest your head on your knees.

Shouts from outside the fortress jolt you awake. You dart into the watchtower and up the stairs. Outside the fortress wall, the warriors are fighting with their hands, thrusting with spears and knives, and swinging the deadliest weapon of all—heavy clubs studded with obsidian blades.

contemporary Maya worry dolls

From a pouch, you take Itzel's worry dolls. You immediately feel calmer about what's happening below. The warriors who survive will return to Tikal and receive special tattoos. The spirits of those who die on the battlefield will receive special care from the gods.

You are left with just one worry. If Tikal and Uaxactun are defeated, what will Calakmul do with a royal prisoner like you?

THE END

To follow another path, turn to page 13.
To learn more about the Maya Civilization,
turn to page 101.

"What if we avoid war by showing our power?" you say. "An ally could help us appear larger and more dangerous."

Itzel nods thoughtfully.

"We could reach out to Waka," you suggest. The kingdom is much smaller than Tikal. But it's located along a route used by obsidian and jade traders, making it wealthy and powerful.

"I'll call up a team of nobles to deliver gifts to Waka as a symbol of friendship," Itzel says. "With an ally like them, Calakmul will think twice before attacking us."

A few days later, a procession of nobles from Waka approaches the palace. Servants carry loads of rich gifts for Itzel.

"Now it's time to prove we're worthy allies," Itzel tells you. "We must head to the ball court to impress Waka. We will demonstrate the strength and skill we'd show on the battlefield."

You sit near Itzel in the viewing stand. She is surrounded by nobles from Tikal and Waka. As in all ball games, the gods are also watching.

As both teams prepare for the game, Itzel turns to you.

"We will prove Tikal's people are strong, clever, and brave," she says, sounding like a determined leader. Then she asks a surprising question: "You're the best companion to me, cousin. You're the kind of player every team needs. Will you play now?"

You've grown up training on this court. But you've never played a game where there is such risk—and so much at stake.

If you play and your team wins, Waka will view Tikal as a valuable ally. But if you play and lose, Waka will search for other allies. Tikal will be forced to face Calakmul alone.

If you decide not to play, turn to page 64.
If you decide to play, turn to page 66.

"I'm flattered, cousin, but one player can't guarantee a victory," you say to Itzel. "Even the twin gods Hunahpu and Xbalanque needed each other to win."

Itzel looks down at the court and nods. Tikal's players look like a pack of jaguars ready to pounce. Headdresses wear snarling faces with green jade eyes. Black paint turns their skin into spotted fur.

Waka's team faces yours. Headdresses turn the players into snakes with fangs and long tongues. Shiny feathers cover their bodies like scales.

The ball is in the air! Both teams dash forward at once.

Thwack! The rubber ball smacks off leather padding on players' hips and cotton padding on their chests. The teams lunge and dive, working together to keep the ball in the air and in their possession.

Waka's players move together like the scales of a single serpent. The ball bounces rapidly between their bodies. Then it bounces off a curved wooden yoke resting on a player's waist and something extraordinary happens.

The ball soars toward the small stone ring mounted high on the court wall—and through it! The hole is barely larger than the ball. Scoring a point like this means an instant win for Waka. The game is over so quickly.

Under the quetzal headdress, Itzel's face has gone pale. She stands up from her jaguar throne and turns away from the ball court.

"With this quick defeat, Waka will not stand with us against Calakmul," Itzel says grimly to her advisors. "But the gods will favor us again one day. Until then, we must train— not for ball games but for war."

THE END

To follow another path, turn to page 13.
To learn more about the Maya Civilization, turn to page 101.

With your heart pounding, you rush down the viewing stand toward the court. You must play—for your cousin and for Tikal.

You quickly strap on padding to protect your shoulders and ribs. You slide a curved wooden yoke around your waist to help launch the rubber ball. It weighs as much as a medium-sized pumpkin.

The game begins! Players grunt as they strike the ball with their bodies. Their shouts echo off the stone walls.

Your teammates are older, bigger, and stronger than you. You feel like you're playing alongside ferocious jaguars. Meanwhile, Waka's team writhes around you like vicious snakes.

You feel Itzel's eyes on you. You cannot let her and Tikal down!

A hoop from a ballgame court at the ruins of Chichén Itzá in Mexico

Darting low through the players, you travel unnoticed around the court. You think of the feathers in your cousin's headdress. Now you understand the creature's power. Its blue-green color allows it to travel invisibly through a forest full of predators.

Waka's players only see you when it's too late. Over and over, you pop up around the court, passing the ball to stronger teammates. They launch it high, while Waka's players fumble.

Tikal wins, but Waka's team fought bravely to the end. Calakmul would be foolish to face them together on the battlefield. There is much to celebrate!

Nobles head to a royal hall for a ceremony. Meanwhile, a great feast will soon take place on the great plaza. Where will you go to honor the new alliance?

If you go to the feast, turn to page 68.
If you attend the ceremony, turn to page 69.

At the feast, you share a cup of frothy chocolate with your teammates. It's the same drink offered to warriors returning from battle. But as you look around, you realize your opponents are nowhere to be found.

Moments later, a nobleman bursts in. "A messenger has arrived with news from Waka!" he shouts. "Waka's ajaw and a princess from Calakmul have decided to marry."

The victory on the ball court melts away. Waka will be Calakmul's ally instead of yours.

Just days later, in a forest outside Tikal, you face another team from Waka—this one armed with obsidian blades. As Calakmul's army charges, you hope the quetzal spirit will guide you again. And if not, at least you have the comfort of knowing that dying in battle is a special honor.

THE END

To follow another path, turn to page 13.
To learn more about the Maya Civilization, turn to page 101.

You head to the royal hall for the ceremony and see a cloth covering a large object. Two of Itzel's advisors pull the cloth away, revealing a stone slab taller than anyone in the room.

The carving on the stone is fresh. It shows Itzel and Waka's ajaw standing face-to-face. Itzel—with her quetzal headdress—has been carved next to Waka's ruler. A spotted jaguar and a feathered snake appear next to them. The ajaws are exchanging gifts of jade objects and weapons.

This stone records an agreement: Tikal and Waka will support each other in trade and war. It will join others that record important events in Tikal's history.

You feel proud of your cousin. Now she has this carved stone to prove she's not just a royal daughter but an ajaw shaping Tikal's future.

THE END

To follow another path, turn to page 13.
To learn more about the Maya Civilization, turn to page 101.

Chapter 4
THE DARKEST SHADOW

The midday sun blazes down on your home city-state of Palenque, a center for astronomy in the Maya Civilization. A hot breeze blows from the palace's courtyard into the workshop. You sit at a low desk, dipping a brush into a curved shell full of black paint.

You carefully draw a symbol—or glyph—onto paper. These glyphs can represent words, ideas, and sounds. Patterns of circles and dots represent numbers. You must memorize hundreds before your training as a scribe is complete. As one of the few people who can read and write in Palenque, you'll be responsible for writing about history, stories about the gods, and astronomy.

Turn the page.

"Look, Yaluk!" your sister Lahun whispers to you from her nearby desk. She holds up her work for you to admire. She's finished covering papers made from bark with smooth, white plaster. They fold up neatly into an accordion-style book called a codex.

"Come, students!" your teacher suddenly calls from the courtyard. His tone is urgent.

Everyone stops what they're doing and hurries outside. The teacher is sitting under a tree with a brush, paint, and a blank paper.

"This lesson is very important," he says, painting a sun glyph. Then he adds black and white shapes on either side. "This glyph is night battling day."

As you stare down at your teacher's paper, you notice something else. The light coming through the tree's leaves is making crescent shapes on the ground.

"What's wrong with the sun?" asks Lahun.

"It's a solar eclipse—the sun is broken," the teacher answers with a mixture of excitement and fear. "Our calendars predicted this, just as they predict lunar eclipses."

You've seen the moon turn red during a lunar eclipse. You've heard it turns the color of blood because a great jaguar is attacking it. But what's happening now, when the sun should be powerful and undefeatable, seems far scarier.

Every night, the sun god, Kinich Ahau, travels down to Metnal, the land of the dead. The sunrise every morning is proof he survived the journey. So why is the sun losing a battle with night in the middle of the day?

The Maya believed Kinich Ahau controlled the sun.

Turn the page.

"Go to the watchtower as the sun dims!" the teacher tells everyone. "And let's pray the gods allow the sun to return and life to continue!"

You're afraid to watch the eclipse, but you know that scribes pay close attention to what's happening in the sky. They use their knowledge to tell farmers when to plant, priests when to hold ceremonies, and even ajaws when to wage war.

The watchtower within the palace would provide the clearest view of the sky. Or you could find a place less frightening for you and Lahun to watch the eclipse. Where will you go?

To climb the palace's watchtower, turn to page 75.

To search for your own special place to watch the eclipse, turn to page 90.

Lahun races up the steep steps of the watchtower ahead of you. You stop at each landing to peek out the narrow windows. The sunlight is dimming right before your eyes.

"I'll beat you to the top!" Lahun's voice echoes off the stone walls.

The room at the top of the watchtower has wide windows. You can see across Palenque's red temples, plazas, ball court, and fields. The sky hangs like a dome all around you.

Astronomers and scribes are already here watching the sky. They're writing on fine paper

Turn the page.

Maya astronomers used watchtowers and elevated platforms to observe the sky and mark the seasons.

made of deerskin covered with plaster. The sweet smell of burning copal incense makes it feel like you're interrupting a ceremony.

Lahun tugs you back toward the stairs. "I want to go," she says.

But the light is dimming, and you're too curious about what will happen next. Strange sounds rise from the forest below. Birds are making their going-to-bed sounds. Insects and frogs are singing their night music. It's the middle of the day, yet twilight is falling. You are frightened to see nature behave so strangely—and amazed that astronomers knew this event was coming.

Lahun squeezes your arm, and you sense her fear. You could stay in the watchtower to see the eclipse. Or you could go down into the palace to avoid the frightening sight.

To stay in the watchtower, turn to page 77.
To escape into the palace, turn to page 79.

"To be scribes, we must understand everything happening in the sky, Lahun," you say. "It's scary when the moon turns red during a lunar eclipse. But we've watched those. And now we'll watch our first solar eclipse."

The landscape below the tower glows with ghostly light. You feel trapped in a frightening dream.

"Shadow snakes!" Lahun cries, pointing to the plaza below.

Eerie shadows are rippling across the stone. The sun quickly dims, and it seems as though Metnal is swallowing the bright, familiar world forever. The air turns chilly as darkness falls. It's as if a great torch has burned out and left behind a cold room.

But in the dark sky—so blue just moments ago—you see stars twinkling. One light is so bright and familiar, you point it out to your sister.

Turn the page.

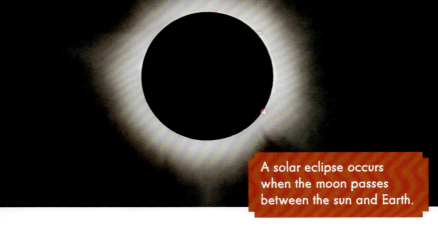

A solar eclipse occurs when the moon passes between the sun and Earth.

"There's Chak Ek, as brilliant as ever," you tell Lahun. Together you gaze up at the familiar light of the star.

"Now Chak Ek is fading—the sun must be getting brighter!" Lahun exclaims.

You remember your teacher's firm warning to protect your eyes. "Don't look at it, Lahun!" you say.

But you're so curious to watch the sun peek out of the moon's shadow. You wonder if just a peek won't hurt your eyes.

If you peek at the eclipse, turn to page 81.
If you keep your eyes covered, turn to page 83.

"Let's leave the eclipse to the astronomers and scribes," you say, leading your sister away.

Reaching the courtyard, you and Lahun rush through the eerie light into the palace. Navigating its maze of corridors, you stop outside a special room. Inside is a wooden chest. It contains a great treasure—a collection of books. Each codex holds writings about history, astronomy, religion, and more.

You lift the chest's heavy lid and search the books until you find a calendar. Carefully, you open the codex. You feel pride gazing at the vivid colors and elegant black lines. This is the work of your elders and ancestors.

You don't have enough training to read it easily. But you recognize some glyphs.

"There's the flower representing the sun," you tell Lahun. "And there's the moon glyph—round like it is at its fullest. See the four-pointed star shape inside that glyph over

Turn the page.

there? It stands for Chak Ek." The bright star is often visible just before sunrise or after sunset.

These glyphs appear in repeating patterns, showing that the sun, moon, stars, and planets move in predictable cycles. Suddenly, you spot the eclipse glyph among them—this must mean that eclipses happen in cycles too!

Barking suddenly echoes through the corridor. A small dog runs past the doorway. Like the wild animals outside, it must be confused by the eclipse.

You and Lahun jump up and race after the dog. But the corridor splits in two directions, each leading underground. One way leads to a dark set of stairs. The other leads to a long ramp. Which way did the dog go?

If the dog leads you to the dark stairway, turn to page 85.

If the dog leads you to the ramp, turn to page 87.

You squint at the sun and feel your eyes immediately start to tear up. You struggle to keep your eyes open as the light grows more intense.

Cheers fill the watchtower and rise from the city. Howler monkey calls rise from the forest, like they do every morning at sunrise.

"The sun is fixed, Yakul!" your sister cries happily. "Look at the red temples against the green jungle and blue sky. It's so beautiful!"

But you don't see that. Everywhere you look, your eyes see shadows and eerie colors. They throb with a terrible, stinging pain.

"Come on, let's go celebrate!" says Lahun.

Your sister dashes down the stairs toward the music starting up in the plaza. You try to follow but stumble. Even though the sun is shining, your vision is dim and blurry. You attempt to focus on the steep stone steps, but black spots float in the center of your vision.

Turn the page.

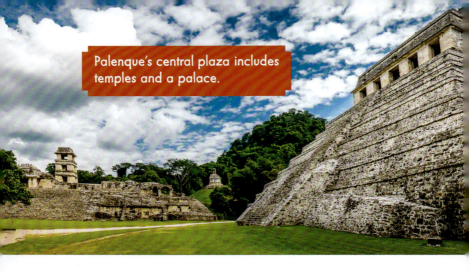

Palenque's central plaza includes temples and a palace.

Finally, you reach the plaza. Everyone is talking about how the sun fought back the darkness. But for you, the world is slowly dimming. How could you be so foolish as to look into the face of the sun god? And how will you do scribe's work if your sight never returns?

When your hand brushes against tall carved stones standing in the plaza, you feel relief. You will learn to read these glyphs by touch and carve them too.

THE END
To follow another path, turn to page 13.
To learn more about the Maya Civilization, turn to page 101.

As the sky brightens once again, you and Lahun fight the urge to look. Instead, you stare down at the city streets. People are crowding toward the ball court.

"Let's go," you say. "A ball game will start soon! The gods will be watching. This is how we thank them for repairing the broken sun."

You and your sister go to the viewing stand. Drumbeats announce the start of the game, echoing across the court. Excitement ripples through the crowd as the ball launches high. Players crouch with tense muscles, waiting for their chance to prove their skill.

As the ball bounces and flies, you explain the ceremony to Lahun. "That moving ball symbolizes the sun that comes up in the east, crosses the sky, drops down in the west, and disappears into night," you say.

"Look out, here it comes!" Lahun shouts as the ball shoots up after two players collide.

Turn the page.

The dark rubber ball sails along a straight path toward you. You crouch and hold your breath. Every pair of eyes in the city shifts to you. This ball has flown off course. But like the sun in the sky, it must stay in constant motion! If the ball bounces to the ground, it means failure. The gods may shake their heads in disappointment—or even anger.

You jump to meet the ball. The heavy rubber smacks your hip and bounces away back to the court. Cheers erupt from every direction.

"You saved the sun, Yakul!" Lahun cries.

You're relieved the ball is back in the game. You're even more relieved that after the eclipse, the sun is setting in the west as usual.

THE END

To follow another path, turn to page 13.
To learn more about the Maya Civilization,
turn to page 101.

A burning torch on the wall lights the staircase leading underground. The dog has disappeared into the darkness.

You take the torch hanging in the corridor. Together, you and Lahun use its light to descend the stairs.

"I hear water," Lahun says. "Are you sure this isn't one of those dark, deep rivers that leads to the land of the dead?" Her frightened voice echoes over and over.

"Oh, no—our engineers built the tunnel," you say. "It collects water from rivers and heavy rains and carries it where we need it, like to the sweat bath and the public fountain."

"There's our little companion!" Lahun shouts suddenly.

The little dog is lapping at the edge of a dark, flowing river. But as you watch, it loses its footing and tumbles in! Lahun dashes over and reaches for the dog.

Turn the page.

"Help me!" she calls. Then she slips in too!

You drop the torch onto the steps and plunge into the water. Using all your strength, you push your sister—with the dog in her arms—back toward the stone stairs.

Lahun turns and holds out a hand to you, but she's not strong enough to pull you up. Your feet and hands slip on the smooth stone walls of the tunnel. The water pulls you away from the flickering torch light of the stairs.

The darkness is so complete that you're confused. Is this the path to Metnal? You drift along, hoping that your body will one day be found in this complex network of tunnels and put to rest in a proper tomb.

THE END

To follow another path, turn to page 13.
To learn more about the Maya Civilization,
turn to page 101.

A ramp leads you down toward a cave-like room. Thick steam billows from inside. This is the royal sweat bath.

"Wait, it's too dark in there!" you shout.

But it's too late. The dog runs ahead, and Lahun follows.

You have no choice but to follow too. Inside, the steam is so thick that it feels like you've entered a strange, ghostly world. You can only make out the orange glow of coals at the far end of the room.

"Yaluk, where are you?" your sister calls.

A Maya steam bath, also called a sweat bath

Turn the page.

You try to make your way toward her voice but bump your shin against a stone bench.

"Ouch!" you exclaim.

"Who's there?" a stranger's voice booms through the steam. "This is no place for children!"

You freeze. You don't know who the voice belongs to, but it doesn't sound welcoming. Lahun runs into you as she races toward the door, the dog racing at her heels.

A loud hiss fills the room behind you just as you escape back through the doorway. For a moment, you imagine a giant snake gliding after you. Then you realize what it is—the stranger splashed water over rocks piled on the glowing coals. Priests must be using the steam bath today. The steam cleans their body and spirit so they are ready to lead ceremonies. Today, they must do all they can to beg the gods to return the sun.

When you emerge outside, you can't believe your eyes. Sunshine bathes the courtyard once again!

On the red steps of a nearby temple, you see the ajaw's enormous headdress. It rises high above the group of priests. Incense smoke floats above the group, rising like a long feather toward the sky.

You decide to create your own ceremony to celebrate the sun. You reach down for a sharp stick. Holding it like a brush, you draw the lines of the sun glyph in the dirt. Then you pass the stick to Lahun. She smiles and adds the dot to the center. The sun god has emerged victorious once again, and you feel as happy as the dog rolling on the warm ground nearby.

THE END

To follow another path, turn to page 13.
To learn more about the Maya Civilization,
turn to page 101.

Together, you and your sister turn and dash through the palace corridors. But Lahun suddenly halts beneath the face of a snarling jaguar carved above a pointed doorway. In the dimming light, the jaguar seems to glow.

"Everything looks so eerie," Lahun says.

"The jaguar is like a warrior," you tell your sister. "It's a powerful climber and swimmer. It moves with stealth and fears no other animal. Kinich Ahau, the sun god, takes its form to survive the nightly journey across the land and bring us the sunrise."

"Then we should watch the eclipse at the temples on the hill," says Lahun. Her fear has turned to excitement.

"We could also go to the ball court," you say. "Every game is a battle between light and darkness—like the eclipse itself."

If you go to the temples, turn to page 91.
If you go to the ball court's viewing stand, turn to page 94.

You hurry toward the temples spread across a hill. Their red color looks dull in the ghostly light. But torches are glowing brightly inside one—a ceremony is taking place.

"What's happening in there?" Lahun asks.

You know the temple faces east to meet the sunrise. Sunlight shines through the doorways. Priests measure the angles of the sunbeams inside and use astronomy to help keep calendars.

"That's the perfect place to ask the gods to fix the sun," you answer.

You and Lahun move closer. Smoke floats into the sky as priests burn paper messages.

"How do the gods answer?" Lahun asks.

You know scribes paint scenes with curved lines and glyphs coming out of the mouths of gods as they speak to the ajaw. But you don't know the answer to your sister's question.

Turn the page.

"The only response we need right now is for day and night to go back to normal," you tell Lahun.

A chilly wind blows as the eclipse turns the afternoon into twilight. The temple now looks like a shadowy mountain. The burning torches at the top look like fire from a volcano.

But then you realize the fire is spreading. The wind is blowing the burning paper across the land.

"They look pretty—like fireflies," Lahun says as she jumps up to try to catch one of the pieces of burning paper.

"They'll burn you, Lahun!" you say, rushing after her.

A spark lands in dry grass near the base of the temple. It quickly leaps up into a flame that grows bright as a torch. The gusting wind created by the eclipse spread the flames higher and brighter.

"Let's run back home!" Lahun says. "Our home is made of stone. We'll be safe there."

Your sister is right, but most of the city's people live in houses made with wooden beams and roofs of grass. Flames quickly leap from one grass roof to another. People are fleeing the city to safety.

Even safe inside a stone palace, you and your family cannot survive in an empty city. You depend on the weavers, potters, farmers, traders, builders, and everyone else who makes everyday life possible. There's nothing you can do but pray to the rain god Chaac to bring a downpour.

THE END
To follow another path, turn to page 13.
To learn more about the Maya Civilization, turn to page 101.

When you arrive at the ball court's viewing stand, a small crowd has gathered.

"It's our teacher!" Lahun exclaims.

Your teacher waves you over. "I'm glad you found us," he says. He's brought paper and a piece of charcoal for sketching, as he does when teaching a lesson.

You take a seat and study the sky. It is now so dark that night insects are chirping. Will it ever be blue again?

"Imagine the sun moving across the sky like a ball in a game," says the teacher, drawing a circle in charcoal.

"So the players are helping the sun fight against the dark?" Lahun asks. "Is that why the court is covered with skulls, bats, and owls?"

"Exactly! Look here." Your teacher draws two stepped shapes squeezing the circle between them. "This is the ball court glyph. It's similar to this one."

He pulls out a sheet with the sun trapped between dark and white shapes—the eclipse glyph. It looks like a ball caught between the sloping sides of a ball court.

"Who will win the battle against darkness now?" another student asks.

As if the sun god heard the question, light and warmth gradually return. The purple sky feels like dawn. Darkness has been defeated on the ball court in the sky!

You hear the sounds of large crowds filling the great plaza. An exciting event must be about to take place. But your teacher is drawing something else, and you are curious to see it. Do you watch over your teacher's shoulder or join the crowd rushing into the plaza?

> To stay and see what your teacher is drawing, turn to page 96.
>
> To go to the great plaza, turn to page 98.

You study the drawing on your teacher's paper. What does it mean?

"Did you notice that small, brilliant light shining when the sun darkened?" your teacher asks. "That's Chak Ek." He begins sketching Chak Ek's star-shaped symbol, a four-pointed star. "He's one of the brightest lights in the sky. Astronomers track his path as closely as the sun or moon."

"He's the brother of the sun god, Kinich Ahau," you say.

"That's right," your teacher replies. "But these brothers are very different. They fight whenever they are near each other. The sun god gives us food, warmth, and life. Chak Ek is the god of war. He dresses like a warrior, carries a spear, and attacks his brother."

"So the eclipse was a terrible battle for the sun god," you say. "He was so weak that Chak Ek must have thought he could destroy him."

Carvings in the ruins of Chichén Itzá show Chak Ek, the Maya god of war.

The teacher nods and lifts his paper. He's drawn eclipse symbols at the top. Under them, Chak Ek dives down through the sky. It looks like he's launching a fierce attack!

"Nature is full of opposites," he says. "Night and day. War and peace. Destruction and creation. We must see the balance, even when it's difficult. That is why we must honor Chak Ek as we honor Kinich Ahau."

You look up to find Chak Ek, but the sun is so bright you must squint. Kinich Ahau has defeated his brother—at least for now.

THE END

To follow another path, turn to page 13.
To learn more about the Maya Civilization, turn to page 101.

You and Lahun race to the crowded plaza. Thousands of people are there, looking up at the temple perched at the top of Palenque's tallest pyramid.

Just then, the ajaw steps out of the temple's entrance. The cloud of burning incense surrounding him makes it look as if he's floating above the pyramid's nine layers, built to reflect the nine levels of Metnal.

"The ajaw must have been conducting a special ceremony inside during the eclipse," you tell your sister.

"So, he fixed the sun!" Lahun said.

"But it's about to be swallowed again," you say, watching thick clouds slide across the sky.

Rain starts to fall, and wind starts to gust. Hail pelts your eyes and skin. The darkening afternoon feels frightening after the solar eclipse. People want to get home, and the crowd presses against you in every direction.

You reach out to grab Lahun's hand. "Stay on your feet, no matter what," you tell her.

Lahun nods, but the crowd pushes you both toward the base of the pyramid. You feel your sister slip to the ground. She will be crushed under this sea of bodies!

"Help, Yaluk!" Lahun cries.

You pull her up and push her toward the pyramid stairs. She climbs to safety.

"Come on!" Lahun cries, reaching for you.

But it's too late. The crowd pulls you away. People press in on all sides, and you feel as if you're starving for air. Before you pass out, you catch a final glimpse of your sister. You imagine Lahun, safe and grown, keeping astronomical records in a codex one day. You hope every eclipse will remind her of you.

THE END

To follow another path, turn to page 13.
To learn more about the Maya Civilization, turn to page 101.

Chapter 5

GIFTS FROM THE MAYA

The Maya were masters of architecture, sculpture, engineering, mathematics, astronomy, farming techniques, storytelling, writing, and more. At the civilization's peak, millions of Maya people were living in more than 40 city-states.

So why did the Maya begin moving away from their urban communities in the 700s CE? Experts blame droughts that lasted for years. By 900 CE, almost all major Maya cities—located in present-day northern Guatemala and nearby areas in Mexico, Belize, and Honduras—were deserted. People may have fled north—to cities such as Mayapan and Chichén Itzá in Mexico's Yucatán Peninsula—to escape starvation and wars over limited food.

Spanish invaders—known as conquistadores—began landing ships along Maya territories in the early sixteenth century. Ferdinand Colón—son of Christopher Columbus—had spotted Maya canoes off the coast of present-day Honduras in 1502. The conquistadores were looking for gold and new territories to rule. The steel swords and guns their soldiers carried were far more powerful than the Maya's spears and clubs. The Spanish also carried diseases that were new and deadly for the Maya.

By 1521 CE, the Spanish ruled over much of modern-day Central America. Yet the Maya were not easily defeated. For more than 150 years, the Spanish battled both independent Maya communities and the newly organized, loosely united kingdoms of neighboring Maya villages. The Maya were protected by their remote locations in dense forests. During that time, some of the Maya, particularly in

Guatemala, continued to live traditional lives like their ancestors. The last Maya kingdom to fall under Spanish rule was Nojpetén in 1697.

But the Spanish wanted to conquer more than Maya territory. They enslaved Maya people and forced them to work on farms and in mines. The Spanish also tried to extinguish Maya culture—they destroyed cities and built Catholic churches on top of temples. The Spanish even burned the Maya's precious codex books. Fortunately, four survived. These and

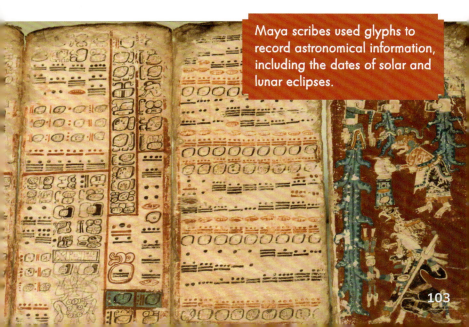

Maya scribes used glyphs to record astronomical information, including the dates of solar and lunar eclipses.

other precious objects, such as pottery and stone carvings, continue to tell the story of the Maya.

Today, an estimated eight million people who can trace their history to Maya ancestors are living in Central America and southern Mexico. This may be close to the population of the Maya Civilization before the Spanish arrived. Some live in farming communities, like their ancestors, while others live modern lives in cities. More than five million speak more than 30 Mayan languages, often in addition to Spanish.

For some people, connecting with ancient Maya culture means heading to the ball court. The game was banned by the Spanish conquistadores in the 1500s. Yet teams today play to keep the ancient game alive. They feel deeply connected to their history when they dress in headdresses, body paint, jewelry, and padding to compete over the heavy rubber ball.

Today, many Maya still play traditional ball games.

Wilberto Canchechan, a player from the village of Ek Balam, Mexico—site of an ancient Maya city-state—told documentary filmmaker Souleyman Messalti about the experience in 2022:

"There is an energy that catches you and surrounds you," Canchechan said. "It feels like we leave our bodies and the ones who are going to play are our ancestors. I am a Mesoamerican ballplayer with a lot of pride."

TIMELINE OF THE MAYA CIVILIZATION

2000 BCE—Farming villages, such as Chalchuapa (in modern-day El Salvador), appear across the Maya Civilization.

1000 BCE—Larger settlements in areas like Copán (in modern-day Honduras) and Chalchuapa (in modern-day El Salvador) form.

600 BCE—The Maya population increases, and cities grow larger. Tikal, one of the Maya Civilization's major city-states, is formed.

300–200 BCE—Mayan writing begins to develop. Maya governments are now ruled by hereditary kings and queens called ajaws.

250 CE—The Maya enter their Classic Period. Cities expand, temples and palaces are built, and populations continue to rise.

562 CE—Tikal is defeated by an alliance of other city-states.

700s CE—Maya people begin to abandon their city-states. Experts believe war, famine, and overpopulation were to blame.

900s CE—The city-state Chichén Itzá rises to power and remains there for 200 years.

1250–1450 CE—After Chichén Itzá is abandoned, Mayapan becomes the most powerful city-state. By the 1450s, it is also abandoned.

1502—Ferdinand Colón—son of Christopher Columbus—spots Maya canoes off the coast of present-day Honduras.

1521 CE—Spanish invaders come to rule over much of modern-day Central America.

1541 CE—Many of the Maya city-states have been conquered by the Spanish. The Maya people continue to resist Spanish rule.

1697 CE—Nojpetén, in present-day Guatemala, is the last Maya city to fall under Spanish rule.

MORE ABOUT THE MAYA CIVILIZATION

>>> The Maya kept three calendars that worked together like gear wheels. One was like a small, fast-moving gear. It marked ceremonies and events. Another calendar—based on a 365-day year—was like a larger wheel turning slowly. It tracked farming cycles and annual festivals. The final calendar, like the largest gear, marked time over thousands of years. These calendars are still used by some Maya communities today.

>>> The Maya crafted beautiful mirrors by polishing stones containing iron. Priests used these highly valuable objects to make predictions about the future. Mirrors were also symbols of authority and power. Nobles and priests used them in ceremonies.

>>> The Maya used dots and bars to represent numbers. They are one of only two ancient cultures to have independently invented the mathematical concept of zero. They represented it with a seashell glyph. It helped them make complex calculations and create accurate calendars.

>>> Maya artists sometimes signed their artwork, which was rare for artists in ancient civilizations in the Americas. The artists added their names to stone carvings and paintings on pottery. They were likely members of the nobility.

THE MAYA CIVILIZATION TODAY

Pottery, books, stone sculptures, buildings, and many other artifacts tell us much about the ancient Maya, but there are still many questions to be answered. Archaeologists—scientists who study human history and culture using artifacts—have carefully cleared away plants and dirt to uncover hundreds of ancient Maya cities. They believe there are likely thousands more in Mexico and Central America. Since 2015, special aircraft have used lasers to detect ancient stone structures hidden by thick forest. This information creates maps of ancient Maya sites yet to be studied.

The ancient Maya site of Joya de Cerén is located in El Salvador.

Stone artifacts tell stories of the lives of the wealthy and powerful in ancient Maya cities. But learning about life in the countryside has been difficult. Villages were made of mud, wood, and grass. These materials don't last like stone. In 1976, archaeologists made a unique find in modern-day El Salvador: a farming village buried by volcanic ash during an eruption in the 600s CE. Archaeologists named it Joya de Cerén. They discovered the shapes of many plants and objects molded inside the volcanic rock.

Many records about Maya culture were created by Spanish conquistadores—the very people who tried to destroy it. For centuries, experts have been learning to read the complex writing system that appears in Maya artwork, architecture, and books. Finally, in the 1950s, a language expert realized that the glyphs are not symbols—instead, they represent sounds or parts of words. Breakthroughs in the 1980s and 1990s allowed scholars to begin sounding out the glyphs with accuracy for the first time. There are more than 800 known Mayan glyphs, and today a few experts can read more than half of them.

The Maya writing system uses glyphs to record sounds and whole words.

Anthropologists—scientists who study people and their cultures—learn about the past by studying the Maya today. Many of their activities—including farming, observing the sky, weaving cloth, making pottery, telling stories, and holding festivals—connect those living today to the lives of their ancient ancestors.

GLOSSARY

adobe (uh-DOH-bee)—a brick made of clay and straw that is dried in the sun

ally (AL-eye)—a person or country united with another for a common purpose

ancestor (AN-ses-tuhr)—a family member who lived a long time ago

architecture (AR-kuh-tek-chuhr)—the designing of buildings

ceremony (SER-uh-moh-nee)—special actions, words, or music performed to mark an important event

drought (DROUT)—a long period of weather with little or no rainfall

hereditary (huh-RED-i-ter-ee)—received or passing by genetic inheritance

incense (IN-sens)—a substance that is burned for its sweet smell, often as part of a religious ceremony

lava (LAH-vuh)—the hot, liquid rock that pours out of a volcano when it erupts

noble (NOH-buhl)—a person of high rank or birth

obsidian (uhb-SID-ee-uhn)—a dark glasslike rock formed by cooling volcanic lava

plaza (PLAH-zuh)—a public square or open space often used for ceremonies

scribe (SKRIBE)—a person who copies books, letters, contracts, and other documents by hand

trench (TRENCH)—a long, deep area dug into the ground with dirt piled up on one side for defense

READ MORE

Eason, Sarah. *The Maya: Fearsome Fighters and Scary Sacrifice*. Shropshire, UK: Cheriton Children's Books, 2023.

Stavans, Ilan. *Popol Vuh: A Retelling*. Brooklyn, NY: Restless Books, 2020.

Yasuda, Anita. *Ancient Civilizations: Aztecs, Maya, Incas!*. White River Junction, VT: Nomad Press, 2019.

INTERNET SITES

BBC: Bitesize: Maya Civilisation
bbc.co.uk/bitesize/topics/zq6svcw

History: Maya
history.com/topics/ancient-americas/maya

National Geographic: Modern Day Maya
education.nationalgeographic.org/resource/modern-day-maya/

Smithsonian National Museum of the American Indian: Maya
maya.nmai.si.edu/maya

ABOUT THE AUTHOR

Danielle Smith-Llera once made a codex for show-and-tell. Her Mexican mother—who grew up near the ancient site of Teotihuacan—suggested using brown paper grocery bags as the bark paper. Before exploring the ancient Maya world, Danielle wrote about 15th century Taíno culture in what is now the Dominican Republic, as well as about Cherokee, Muscogee, Chumash, and other Indigenous nations carrying on their ancestors' traditions today. Danielle has written nearly 40 books during her family's many moves between Washington, D.C., and government posts in Belgium, India, Jamaica, Romania, and the United Kingdom.

BOOKS IN THIS SERIES

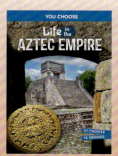
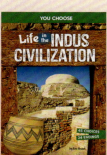
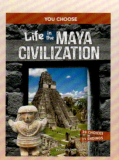
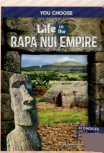